War Bird

PHOENIX POETS

DAVID GEWANTER

*War Bird*

THE UNIVERSITY OF CHICAGO PRESS
*Chicago & London*

DAVID GEWANTER is professor of English at Georgetown University. He is the coeditor of Robert Lowell's *Collected Poems* (2003), and the author of two books of poems, *In the Belly* (1997) and *The Sleep of Reason* (2003), both published in the Phoenix Poets series by the University of Chicago Press.

The University of Chicago Press, Chicago 60637
The University of Chicago Press, Ltd., London
© 2009 by The University of Chicago
All rights reserved. Published 2009
Printed in the United States of America
18  17  16  15  14  13  12  11  10  09      1  2  3  4  5

ISBN-13: 978-0-226-28978-6 (paper)
ISBN-10: 0-226-28978-8 (paper)

Library of Congress Cataloging-in-Publication Data
Gewanter, David.
    War bird / David Gewanter.
        p. cm. — (Phoenix poets)
    Poetry.
    Includes bibliographical references.
    ISBN-13: 978-0-226-28978-6 (alk. paper)
    ISBN-10: 0-226-28978-8 (alk. paper)
    I. Title.  II. Series: Phoenix poets.
    PS3557.E897W37 2009
    811'.54—dc22                          2008049199

*for* RUTH GEWANTER

*ruthless and fiery pacifist*

Not for nothing are ye called the Free People.
Ye have fought for freedom, and it is yours.
    Eat it, O wolves.

Rudyard Kipling, *The Jungle Book*

# CONTENTS

THREE: WAR BIRD

# ACKNOWLEDGMENTS

My thanks to the editors of the magazines and Web sites in which these poems first appeared:

*Agni* Online: "In again Out again"
*Fulcrum*: "Break-Up Café," "Mistress Umlaut," "1972: The Battery"
*Literary Imagination: The Review of the Association of Literary Scholars and Critics*: "Cook at Maui," "Surrey: Walled Garden"
*New Ohio Review*: "Pediment"
*Poetry*: "Hamlet of Merano: The Lotus Eaters," "The Old Parables"
*Poetry International*: "Baudelaire's Day Book"
*Slate* (www.slate.com): "Against the Grain"
*The Threepenny Review*: "Three at 4:43"
*Tikkun: A Bimonthly Interfaith Critique of Politics, Culture & Society*: "Body Text"
*TriQuarterly*: "War Bird: A Journal"

Thanks also to the Mrs. Giles Whiting Foundation, to Georgetown University's faculty fellowship, and to my family and friends; all have supported this project.

# THE OLD PARABLES

Nature, not emotion, has creased
the dolphin's smile—yet she
   so adores

the mariner, she kicks to keep
her snout above water, the sun
   drilling her blind—

A coral reef, blooming toward
the light: skeletal calcite
   fathers

fatten the towers, and push
the ocean water still higher,
   shading them—

Sink before me, dear friends,
feud and fuse, join the chafing
   bone rung

ladder I clamber up, friend
on friend, lest the hissing foam
   freeze my jaw—

# One

## Day Book

# IN AGAIN OUT AGAIN

Put words on the move,
    on the make, make
your body move in hard play,

game

of hoops, or sex, *the low post*
    *reaching in, going back door,*
*up and down, the double pump—*

winter locker room

wet from boys changing,
    wrestlers in martian
sweatsuits spitting

into cups

to make their weight,
    b-ball players shambling
aboard the team bus, one styling

a Mao hat, one

Detroit porkpie & fedayeen scarf
    and, sitting next to me
one Fruit of Islam soldier cap

*Hey*

*my brother from New York,*
    *check this comic:* free from
YOUR BLACK MUSLIM BAKERY,

the Honorable

Elijah Muhammad's
    prophetic 'toon, flying saucers
circling earth zapping every

White Man—

my fellow guard laughing
    "now that's you right here,
that's the jews," little

black-ink white

men plummeting from a bank;
    he played the Last Poets
*The REVoLUtion*

*will NOT*

*be TELevised*, I played
    *The Rite of Spring*, our bus
chuffing past *Nerfertiti's*

*Hubcap World*

and *Diamond Dialysis Center*—
    We'll lose tonight's game,
our baby sky hooks drop

below the basket, the rim

that once grabbed the wedding
    ring of a man dunking
and flayed his finger,

the skin

hanging from the rim,
    a ladies' pale glove—
One blood under flesh,

under

a marriage that goes
    up and down, that dives
for the loose ball,

lightfooted comedy

weighted and doomed like
    the never-scoring oldtime player
*In again Out again*

*Finnegan,*

a dribbling Onan, desire's shadow
    moving below the orbital
Dr. J and Butterbean Love

who

even as intern and seedling
    were guarding us—
our fragrant Black saints

scorching the mid-air,

stars forever blind to us, buoyant,
    kettle-hard piñatas
hoisted above the court

and out of reach.

# BODY TEXT

"CLOSE COVER BEFORE STRIKING"—Acme Matches

Toe speckled with blood, sour blush of spirit;
the villager's thumb smashed blue

 from hammering evil thoughts into
 the Yoruba totem doll:

his marble eye and smile of bone
float above the indigestible belly

 of griefs that the townsfolk
 feed him, nail by nail. . . .

A baby fights gravity to stand; her body
lists and yaws, begins its life of self-correction

 so that later, if she slashes her wrists
 and chokes down all the pills—

still, they are anti-coagulants;
she wakes up alive but scabby.

 Unversed in poetic justice,
 the body forgives

but can't forget. We used to read it slowly:
during the ancient wars, a messenger

    could dawdle weeks in camp
    until his hair grew back,

hiding the map tattooed on his scalp.
Now we pay for our figures:

    when the dictator proclaims
    "the future's in your hands,"

rebels chop off a thousand arms,
asking the victims, "short sleeve or long sleeve"—

    Can our bodies turn innocent again?
    We have cleansed ourselves, planting

crimes in the spongy flesh of our teachers:
open to our mistakes, their skin absorbs

    every fault, a body's true instruction:
    the botched colon and missing period,

the "terminally disorganized
Appendix"—: Our problems plump

    their calf and moon, their dimpled
    pedimental haunches that

waggle up the schoolhouse stairs,
these simple men of Hobbes, swimming against

   a student whaleherd of Rousseau—
   In summer, teachers moonlight

as customs inspectors . . . credulous,
starved for human histories, they swallow

   cock and bull tales, and let through
   the satchelfuls of drugs

that later dim their students—
Tonight, older than the yearbook images

   gaping back at us, we compose ourselves
   in sleep, walking the error of our ways

amidst the smiling, still handsome
schoolmasters of our youth, now voided of us.

   Knowledge settles back like dust
   inside the mouth, blue dust of berries

by night, bleaching at dawn
to fine chalk, or ash.

# HAMLET OF MERANO: THE LOTUS EATERS

The small Alps, the frilled, puritanical
collars of snow, melting in the sun of Italy—

heroes drift here: they kill for high ground,
grow lazy and forgetful, then give the land away . . .

This hamlet, Merano, belongs to Italy

for now, but in its Prussian piazza stands
the bust of Maria Theresa, pragmatic

lady-King of Hungary, and Austrians
squeeze inside the gingerbread

beer and pasta houses, burbling Italian
to waiters who click back perfect German—:

Everyone here is exiled, or prays that
beer is oxygen, and that the starched,

health spa fräulein will walk the cobbles
of your spine . . .

Wander upstream, walk against its time,
find the true hamlet of Tirol,

where the ageless dirndled Mary, princess
de Rachewiltz, sprints the castle stairs

to serve high tea, and talk of Pound her father:
"*Pound loved all people*," she breathes,

and kisses her guest hotly.

His walking stick and hat pose downstairs;
the castle's "Agrarian Technology" exhibit

awaits the fall of capitalism; the ox-eyed
girls of Appalachia College (study abroad)

stretch for the castle's champagne grapes,
or play hacky sack in short-shorts . . .

O to be a grape underfoot—:

even Kafka, scowling like Bogart,
came to Merano once, *for the waters*:

giddy, he pranced through
the Hotel *Palace Schloss Maur*,

writing Hamlet backward, *Tel Mah*, tell
Queen Gertrude: the one-act play with no revenge . . .

The girls' skin is browned butter,
unmarked, unreadable;

where are the rashes?—

Pound had shipped Mary maple saplings
to spark industry in maple syrup,

*"you'll make a killing"*—
the tree-boxes also hid sprouts of

poison ivy, which spread like locusts
through the Alps. But now no rash.

The eye sees what it remembers,
the imagination dreams its rut

is fresh, not tragical-comical-historical. . . .
Who, pocketing the chilly grapes, would not

name himself king here,
and forget who is king?

# BREAK-UP CAFÉ

*Table by*   The neat one, the nasty one, the quick one, the wet one,
*window*     a little before breakfast, the midnight plump & bump,
             make-up and break-up sex, sympathy and funeral sex

    *—wait, let me ask you . . .*

down and dirty, doing it on boats, balconies, closets &
    swing sets,
drive-ins or take-outs, masks and hats, soft ropes, little toys

    *—hang on: that's all the sex*
    *you're* NOT *having with him? . . .*

*Armchairs*  My father. This guy hated
             owing favors, he never cut in line;
             he paid off his mortgage early,

then the market dropped; decades later,
he died still waiting for "the bounce"—
Not me: I'll max my second home loan,

then . . . time for another re-fi . . .
Why not live off the house? It makes more
dough than I do. I call it my dad,

15

I hit it up for loans, I'm like
the loser kid who won't move out.
The guy I bought it from looked grown-up,

but I opened up the bedroom closets:
his wife kept so many clothes
he got dressed in the basement.


*Last booth* . . . he comes in asking for Viagra, middle-aged guy,
he's married to a skinny Russian girl,
Internet deal, and she'd been living with five

or ten relatives in a parlor,
and if everyone's gone out, then she can screw
so she's turned on lightning-quick, and getting hers

    *—This sounds like a man's dream come true.*

Exactly! but he's like, "howsabout some wine
and flowers, Honey? Perry Como? Or dinner for two . . ."


*Newspaper* NORFOLK, NEB., SEPT. 29—
*rack*     They walked into the U.S. Bank shooting,
and when they were done, four bank workers
and a customer

were dead.
*There is a lot of disbelief,* said Kelly Loren, 33.
*You live in a small town, you think Omaha, Chicago—
anywhere but here.*

Population
23,500, Norfolk is the birthplace of
comedian Johnny Carson. . . . The violence didn't stop.
On Friday, State

Trooper Zack Mark
killed himself, apparently believing
he could have prevented the shootings.
   A week earlier,

confiscating the handgun
of one of the suspects, Mark copied down
the wrong serial number and didn't discover
the gun was stolen.

The man was
released on bond. Pictures of the dead were hung
neatly in the Knights hallway as residents
dropped donations

and waited patiently
for plates of scrambled eggs, hash browns, and links.


*Counter*    At first it's like dogs—if you point at the moon they'll
look at your finger. Then they put it together. But my
little girl, very literal: when I told her *let's cut through
the building,* she expected a buzzsaw; and she's still
waiting for me to *blow up a picture.* It's fun . . . but then
I lose track, only seeing her on the weekends, and now
she's starting to talk like my ex. . . .

*Couch*    Therapy? I went because my brother's a pathological liar,
I had to play parent, stop his credit cards, all that—

It's made me a good investigator though:
I just think, *what would Peter do?* and catch the guy. . . .

Guess what: my therapist's going senile.
His eyes look flatter lately; or thicker . . . meanwhile,

I make up stories to keep him company—I even sing!
My friends say I'm on a power trip. They're wrong:

in his room I'm talking to everyone I've known. I'm
loading him up: I'll bury my problems with him.


*Back booth*    . . . so why do we call them "practical jokes" anyway—?

—*Practical, that means, it needs an action.*

Ok, but only guys do practical jokes, right? tying a bike rack
to the wedding limo, and it pulls off the car bumper.

—*Or boys do them.*

Or boys do them, ok . . . but not girls. Except for Sandra:
if you piss her off, she'd super-glue your door lock;

she hated her neighbors' wind chime, and cut out
the clapper. Guys loved telling tales

about Sandra, but would never date her—
— *Of course not. Why seduce a girl who loves revenge?*


LOST    *In the sight*
FOUND,    *of the Almighty my mother picked me*
notebook   *off her neck like a leech—*
           *but when night*

           *returns I return to her*
           *as on the day before,*
           *and this becomes our*
           *binding rule: every night she bows down*

           *to the retribution and the yoke.*
           *In the gates of her dream*
           *there is no one*
           *standing but me.*

# BAUDELAIRE'S DAY BOOK

September 1993: the Cauliflower.

My father dying. When I saw him at "the Home," part of his face drooped like soft clay under heat, his cheek a dented pepper. I stepped back and clutched the wall—it was *my* face, my drip of lead above the brow.

He was swinging his arm round and round, helped by a goat-bearded therapist, PEDRO. Rehab? Nothing could strengthen an arm against the tumor gnawing his brain. But therapy justified his stay to the insurers: it paid the attendants, the night staff, catering, maintenance—swing away!

The Hospital nurses had been slim, sardonically cheery, their platform clogs pranced, click clack. But now, the Rest Home ladies. Massive, flat-faced, they hum above the polyester voop-voop of skirts, girdles, stockings & straps, full cups, the beautiful housings . . . My lust desperate, I plump as they bend to fluff a pillow, or inject insulin (they treat his diabetes, sugaring the tumor). *Lean over, Bertha!* I could bed them one by one, a low sour passion born of misery, thankfulness, to prove our family still warm and capable of earnest groping. Instead,

I feed him pulp food, hoist him in the suspended sling, looped to a metal frame on wheels so that one lady can take him from the bed to the wheelchair and back to bed, a bucket of a man, dangling over the empty well. . . . My finger gets caught in the pulley, now blood splatters the chain and sheet. A fragrant nurse hands me a gauze . . . her painted nails, that pattern: the flag of Samoa?

Later I pray to the blister, that my nail would grow and loop and be cut before he dies. I watch for it when I talk to him by phone; at night the nail speck stares back, cloud or blastula moving under the coarse ice.

A previous stroke had made him skin sensitive: doing the crosswords, he idly shaved his arms with an electric razor, whose low-frequency waves grew a cauliflower in the brain-pan; it fattened in its room like an anchorite. No one is to blame, it's time for him to go, the yellowing Rest Home walls slacken and shape themselves for the next man. One day the women didn't come to roll him over, he dialed 911: the ambulance drove round from the front, the emergency guys scolding him, then cursing at everyone.

He died before I could clip it, but I gouged out the nailtop and sealed it in an envelope. A runaround infection came on, the finger bloomed a rainbow of blood, until one day the whole nail came off, a trembling soggy mollusk under a little skull cap. No women now: here at last is my portion.

## DESAPARECIDOS

### MA JOAD

My mother hitchhiking,
the balled-up hand windmilling, crooked thumb
    a fin at her shoulder,
suburban Okie who stops an Impala

    on Martha's Vineyard, gone with
her bag of coffee, chicken lobster, and sweet corn.

### DUET

The year the conk turned to Afro,
greasers grew their freak flags. Then Detroit burned—
    a bump in the lunchroom,
a muttered curse, friends rushing in like

blood to the face—
a race-riot, and handcuffed boys on TV.
    Between classes next day,
the principal pipes out Janis Joplin's

    *Piece of My Heart*
and then James Brown, *I Feel Good*.

WALLED CITY

The hand swoops down
from the ear, putting the face in parenthesis:
    the deaf-sign, in Dutch,
for *woman*, shape of the old snood-cap

from Breughel. But in Florence,
the deaf hand scoops out from the chest—
    *woman*, and round
Italian breasts on show. But only in Florence:

    Bologna uses a different sign,
a Florentine can't signal for women there.


THE UNSPEAKABLE

My student Charlie Bernstein,
strapping, curly hair, about to take a step,
    like Rilke's blind man
pondering, fingers at his lips . . . he wrote poems

about flowers, hillsides,
the girls he would bring there, and I nudged him,
    "send your stuff to the poet
Charles Bernstein, he says language writes his poems,

he says 'that these dimensions
are the material of which the writing'—:
    this guy should meet another
Charles Bernstein. Tell him you wrote his books."

Curse my tongue. The boy
never mailed them, but after he left school
    he was driving all night
through Texas, and a truck killed him.

        —


I met Prof. Bernstein once
(stooped, alive) and told him about Charlie.
    He said _____. And I answered _____.
Two dray horses champing at seeds and forage.

# THE GIANTS' CAUSEWAY

    Boys and girls
from the sodden hip-ferns of Bayhead ridge
settled down in low clay huts. But Finn kept
    growing, from oak legs

    to flaming Irish hair:
Finn the Giant, tossed his father for ten-pins.
*What man have I become?* he asked the seals.
    Could see

    tomorrow's clouds;
could see, on the shores of Scotland, giant
Angus bellow for a fight. *Well, here's a match.*
    So each giant

    massed a stone pier
to bridge the anxious waters. Then came Angus
striding, heaving boulders like seeds before him—
    they fell to the depths,

    a petrified rain
upon Sir Patrick Spens and his weed-rooted
council of drowners, their deaths clutched in
    the moon's bosom,

their dry-eyed
widows ashore. From Ireland, Finn's wife
saw that Angus was bigger. "Finn," she said,
   "Drag your boat-frame

into the kitchen—
find my sewing-box, and lie on this sheet."
When Angus stepped in, a colossal baby
   squawked and rocked

its boat-cradle—
Finn, swaddled. "Don't mind the bairn," she said,
"his daddy will calm him—" What massive man
   could dandle

such a baby?
The kettle shook as Angus, like a bachelor
terrified of family life, galloped the bridge
   back to Scotland, ripping out

the molar rocks
behind him; the Atlantic, unbraced,
washed the sailors' hats to shore, froth at
   the widows' dimpled feet. . . .

In Ireland,
the gristled pier still juts out, a book-end.
Stand in its shadows, feel the salt wind scrape—
   You cannot find

your way home,
but only the first, crazed block of causes. . . .
Finn suckled a thole pin—his wife leapt aboard,
    laughing:


    the skeletal
boat creaked, grinding its notch upon the fabled
sea floor. Two masks, a marriage. Then sleep,
    plummeting


beyond sound or sense.

## BOOK OF THE BLURBERS

after Coetzee

Their caravan never came to our village.
     Still, there was evidence: a mica sheet
   for a mirror, a hollow shell

to carry the voice between towns,

the mutilated scraps of paper
     wheeling at our feet . . . that was all
   we found of the traveling Blurbers,

though the boys ran up

waving bits of cloth,
     "we saw them this time, Uncle, we did!"
   The desert is a gritty sea,

the wind scours a rusty gun turret

to silver, then drowns
     the next gun in a tide of sand—
   our island is this brackish water hole.

Tired of waiting, we waste

our days mocking the old men:
        "What is a banker?
        *The hand of Death.*"

"What is a priest, waiting for God?

*A sailor's wife.*"
        But at night we talk of the Blurbers,
        the unseen, legendary scribes

whose covered Book, our grandfathers say,

carries our wisdom throughout the world.
        Its letters are traced by a bayonet
        dipped in the bowl of the brain:

        THIS IS HOW TO BRAID BREAD.
        THIS IS HOW WE VEIL THE BRIDE.
        THIS IS HOW LAVENDER IS GROUND.
        THIS IS HOW WE VEIL THE WIDOW. . , ,

————

One day a stranger rides into town.

Haltingly, he says, "One of your Blurbers
        came to our city,
        his annual visit, to speechify.

But he died—a natural death, I assure you—

and I bring you his robes, brocades,
and this, your special Book.
We never understood his purpose

and—well, he was mocked:

our own scribes called him *Blabber*,
and said his cattle were
*Oxymorons.*" The Book's pages

were blank except for his notes:

*Let the stranger feed me.*
*I am gone so long from my village,*
*I could not find my café.*

*What of it? What of "My People"?*

*Angels and ghosts.*
*Cityfolk call us simple—but they are*
*the chick that eats the nest.*

*One day I will skip my dreary song,*

*the made up words—*
*and show my stranger-hosts*
*what their country*

*has squeezed from my throat. . . .*

# THREE AT 4:43

for Thom Gunn

Light torn by trees. A café, a girl,
and a gray man. A windstorm must have struck him:
her eyes follow his frayed collars and hair.

Then another girl is talking. "My friends
saw my chili tattoo and called it a carrot—
so I had it removed. Now, a ghost chili carrot."

And here comes my friend, limping on
his heavy boot, the heel come off. A cobbler's shop
appears, and I buy the black nails,
the dwarf's hammer, glue and strapping.

I work hard on it, bending there
until he speaks and walks on.
But as he is dead, his voice and step
make no sound.

## 1972: THE BATTERY

That spring, a heaven-glut of rain—
    towers of it sway and shatter

against the muted homes, draining
    a brown tea from the chimney-hole;

the drunken elms lash the power-lines,
    corrupting the grid, crackle of lights

as two boys clomp the bedroom stairs.
    They pack their tools and chainsaws,

by night they cut down illegal road-signs,
    they are the *Billboard Bandits*,

their tag,   ¡PROPOGANDA, NO! CLEAR THE PATH—
    No one speaks of them at school,

our student council, to fight the CIA,
    burns its records, then disbands.

A spring of shaving cuts, of getting riled
    over nothing, of fever for girls' lips,

or a glance at least, watching their T-shirts
    falter at the neck, or stretch

over nipple, watching for the nipple to stretch. . . .
    The battery hums along the leg,

cockhead shines and fattens, wets the fuse—
    *Hey whats happening?* Unbearable,

this sagging treadmill march to summer,
    then college, then mortgage . . . to become

a nail hammered to the vanishing point
    ten years on, stuck on a block

near your parents' block, near the father
    who once handled Einstein's brain

(kept by the pathologist at Princeton),
    and said, "It felt like every other brain I felt."

For us, ejaculation felt like genius,
    and violence, a form of curiosity,

like jumping backward over a hedge
    on a dare, snapping a rib

on a bike-rack, laughing and crying. . . .
    After days of nervous, sodden heat,

the swirling rain and wind return,
    that in darkness guide the Bandits' ladder

to the power lines. Lightning spoke
    its own truth to power: one boy found gasping,

his legs torched, and his friend, the one
    who carried the charge longer, snuffed out.

*O protectors, cast down your arms.*
    Death conducted: the school flag droops

at half-mast, as it did for last year's Teen Death,
    and teachers shepherd the grieving girls inside

while couples fondle in the sunstruck woods—
    What can we do now? Nothing. And yesterday

we did nothing. . . . Then the news breaks:
    the Cambodia bombing,

and students vote to keep the flag down—
    cheerleaders cry, and loyalist

football-types rebel: they hoist it up,
    ring the flagpole hip to hip, glowering,

a shaven head musk-ox formation,
    while skinny grainfed hippies

race downhill, *The flag! Get the flag!*
    bouncing off the laughing men,

fighting until the pain feels real,
    then toiling uphill to charge again.

*Two*     ·     American Incognito

# JACOPONE *PIETÀ*: JUSTICE

Why, Conscience, do you sleep? You never gave me rest,
your tongue like a razor peeled my root-ball, sin—
    yet now your eyes,
the blaze and curse of my nights, have shut.

*Jacopone, I've watched you burden Justice*
*with your excuses, piling corpses onto the scales*
    *till her thin arms broke.*
*But now you carry her voice, her clear,*

*single verdict—so we can live in peace.*

Then sleep on, haggling Brother. Sleep and starve:
    for you were only born
of my guilt, and you have fed on my sins.


after "Laud 47"

# AMERICAN INCOGNITO

But to whatever animal we ascribe these remains, it is certain
such a one has existed in America, and that it has been the
largest of all terrestrial beings. It should have sufficed to have
rescued the earth it inhabited, and the atmosphere it breathed,
from the imputation of impotence. . . .
—Thomas Jefferson, *Notes on the State of Virginia*

I called for armour, rose, and did not reel.
But when I thought . . .
                              I could feel
My wound open wide.
—Thom Gunn, "The Wound"

## THE STATES

For he can creep.

Whose doctor said his bipolar was pre-existing.
Smacked in the head by a steel cargo door,
hinges tied with a hamburger bag.
The day he blew up: a sucking silence, mouth of tar,
    story told over and over,

bump and rattle, caissons rolling.
The blacked-out school bus window is
scratched to read GHOST RECON. Street signs flash by,
"This here is Georgia. Now I see New Hampshire,
    and here's Colorado." *What country is this city?*

Gorked on pain-relief cocktails, Iraq to Landstuhl Med
to Andrews Air Force, wheelchair bus to Walter Reed.
Wounded when burning poppies, now afloat
on morphine. "As a state," he once emailed,
    "Afghanistan is next to Mars."

The navigator slides along a wall:
"Sir, can you show me *north*?"
Where the gazebo is a tank. Where the manhole covers a bomb.
Who apologize for shaving cuts. Skull plate,
    40-lb. gain from meds, big ox baby.

"Fall in," the heart-attack sergeant tells
the legless men. "At ease," he tells the psychotics.
They limp by drug dealers for their scoop
of Baskin-Robbins. Are told,
    "Suck it up, get used to the outside world."

Who are saved, but die in dreams,
salute with a mechanical arm.

Beneath the marble, beneath the paper laws;
the paved boglands and legs-up taverns,
the slave-built steps of the Capitol. Winter 1898,
a sewer-man digs up a dinosaur spine,
    a *nomen nudum*, naked & unnamed fossil


tombed later at the Smithsonian
near Jefferson's Mammoth tooth
that rattled his pocket, cherished knuckle-bone
and proof against the French naturalist
    who with powdered hands


wrote that New World dampness and cold
had stunted flora, animals, and Man:
the *American Degeneracy*.
Jefferson ordered Lewis & Clark to find
    a living Mammoth,


the "animal de l'Ohio"
grazing somewhere west
of Big Bone Lick, Kentucky, and—
lest a species wither, or Nation grow small—
    brought Mammoth bones to Monticello.


"WHEREAS, the remains of a large carnivorous dinosaur,
which may be an ancestor of the Tyrannosaurus rex,
were found at First and 'F' Streets, SE,

NOW, THEREFORE, I, MAYOR OF THE DISTRICT
OF COLUMBIA, do hereby proclaim January 28, 2001,
as 'CAPITALSAURUS DAY.'"

Anthony A. Williams


DISCOVERY IN SIBERIA

Reindeer of the herdsman Jarkov nuzzle
a tusk frozen 20,000 years. Soon,
French naturalists arrive. Radar shows
the Holy Grail of Mammoth hunters,
    a frigid bulk, twice an elephant's size—

Timber saws cut the block. Hoisted by
military helicopter to Stalin's
gulag caves, frozen labs for scientist-prisoners,
now re-opened. Waving hair-dryers
    to sublimate the ice, so that Discovery

can film them planting clone eggs
inside an elephant, hatching a Mammoth
American defender to split the ramparts,
show scheduled for release in *2001*
    —the year when, in the sci-fi film,

the monkeys learn to talk;
when Mayor Williams greets
the Capitalsaurus and the new President Bush;
when Mohammed Atta decides he
    cannot date a waitress.


SECURITAS

Weary headlands roll through zones of night,
red lights flash the muted streets,
crotch-of-moss draining a blue spark dawn—
We sleep, staring. Tree-shapes and stars prod us,
    the belt of Orion is a martyr's bomb.

And the king, our godsbody, lies abed
groaning, chill spirit belaboring the flesh—
His spit and sperm are tallied; his temperature,
a weather report told by doctors. Until
    lady *Securitas* peers from a cloud—

her bloodlined hands, the blank, bureaucratic face!
We pray with our bodies: cold sweat, a hymn
of twitches, heart racing, shrieking dreams . . .
But fragrant *Securitas* has only
    come for him—

To compass him about.
Lifting out her breast.
Stoppers his mouth with a thick nipple.
Squeezing till the ichor throbs from his eyes,
    milk to make us thirsty—

IRAQ & TEXAS: DJINN ROADS

*Helicopters park at Forward Base* EXXON;
*only the sand is flying today, and it breaks*
*the speed limits, 50 miles an hour. Visibility zero;*
*the air is hot as blood, the sky is burnt amber.*
    Lord keep still our hands.

In Texas, teens patrol the roads by night,
burning the body's fuel—State Troopers pull them over.
George, fishtailing *dauphin*, a graceful
falldown drunk, clouds the breathalyzer:
    FELONY DUI. Daddy's name sinks the report—

Election night, heaven staring, and Laura's
yellowcake Chevy mows down her boyfriend:
VEHICULAR HOMICIDE: the car found guilty.
"I know this as an adult, it was crushing,"
    she recalls. Her scented, unmarked body

sweats beneath foundation garments and paste.
His unmarked body, and fructifying breath,
his stone squint chasing snakes from the sun—
They walk, O my darling, the hill of light;
    the bite of remorse teaches them to bite.

*Then it rains. What falls from the sky is not water*
*but mud, raindrops pulling clouds of sand*
*into large wet globs. "It was biblical," says*
*Col. Gibbs. Lights a cigarette, his back to the storm:*
    *"You've got to embrace the suck."*

*From the dust, the limbs jerk up alive, stagger home*
*to camp. Martian: neck gators for the nose, goggles*
*seal off the eyes, baby wipes.* WHAT DID YOU FIND THERE?
*A slipper, an ear, some wire. A chemical suit.*
  *A map of water.*

———

From Stalin's cave, just bits of gristle—unreadable,
no Frankenstein DNA. They rewrite the *Mammoth* show.

From Walter Reed, "an aggressive campaign
to deal with the mice infestation."
  Recovery rooms, "spit-polish clean."

Whose mother swallows all the soldier medicine.

Who wheels himself in to play *Texas Hold 'Em.*

Whose father says, "It was OK for my son
to give his body. They try in their power,
  but it reverses itself."

Jefferson's *American Incognito*
is ground up for fertilizer—
the maid said it was cow bones. Sweet heartland,
Governor Meriwether Lewis
  of Louisiana, depression pre-existing,

shoots himself in the chest and head.

Who sit by the apples and wingback chairs.
"If I had two hands, I'd order two vodkas"—

Who cannot count his change.
    Who wake up and punch the air.

# PEDIMENT

Like backtalking teenagers sent to their rooms,
    the boyhoods
of husbands dangle in closets, or bulge a locker,
    ancient toys

awaiting the senile hand—here inside the trunk,
    the *Furry Freak Brothers*
rub the benighted sovereignty of
    *Big Ass Comix*

or nuzzle the *Up Against the Wall*
    *Street Journal*, where
a sweaty financier is pictured with a purpley,
    squash-sized penis—

Why grow up? The basement monarch
    palms his relics:
the crumbled essay on pacifism, scrawled
    to the Draft Board's

faustian query, *Let's say you see your mother*
    *being raped.*
*What would you do?* The brochure, "Amputating
    Your Small Toe Safely."

The brochure, "Nudist Communes
    of Canada."
The letters to the war-vet father, chip off
    the old block,

chip on your shoulder, twinkle in
    your daddy's eye
now poked out, that never read them—
    And here, your postcards

of Hogarth's faltering *Rake's Progress*
    spill out, a Tarot
of hokum, of coulda wouldas. Shuffle the cards
    and play a new past,

so that now the coy syphilitic whores
    first dress up Rake
to marry his puckered, humpback bride . . .
    next, after the wedding

he woos her frantically, still proposing
    marriage until,
fed on madness, he hugs the jailhouse floor,
    ecstatic, inert,

a pile of flesh weighing on everyone,
    lazily aping
the dream of man—and yet, in the last card,
    somehow striding

fresh from his cell, fair virgin at the end
    of days, never
ruling a house, never the bloated sugar bee
    hung from the pantries

of the family hive, dry stinger and bellyful
    of beer,
throbbing, a food-sac stroked for jelly. . . .
    The footlocker

clamps shut, hasp, buckle and boy-scout latch.
    A lodestone.
A marble dog at rest beneath
    a marble child.

# MICHELANGELO: THREE POEMS IN BLACK

## SILKWORM

Born in darkness, my coiled spunk of service
dribbles down in heaps from my clenched belly,
endless birthing of white heaps, spun sugar
to spoil the breast and arms of a lady

bending to dab the muck from her shoe—
Oh, to squeeze out this life-thread, to cling
to a breast with my grappling hooks and lines!
As for the snake, that gloomy, self-escaping worm

pops toward the light . . . his raw, startled eyes.
He hates his skin—papery flesh of his flesh.
    Yet what dies from me can never die:

one night, my lady will take me to the grave;
her body will rest inside my seed-thread, inside silk shoes
    (her favorites) that today kiss her feet in the rain—

## SACRED NIGHT

Cavern and grotto, the blind palace-vault—
all day it guards the Night from sun's explosions,
from pick-axe and shovel jabbing sunlight
into the soil. . . . Sleepless, Night wanders the hall

and chamber: *What's this?* What does she fear?
—not the sun, the cyclops waiting at the cave,
but the lone candle or pulsing glow-worm
whose light will bring her Empire down. The earth

bakes, decays; the chaste sun plays father to
swelling moulds, to grubs that burst and smear
 the plowman's blade—the plowman himself

a breeding ground and tomb. His noon-shadow
puddles at his feet, darkness always serving him—
 His bristling root that sinks the Monarch's thigh.


WORDS AT NIGHT

The charity of sleep,
     that turns me to stone,

not to see, not to feel
     the world's broken body

hardening, unashamed—
     What freedoms inside a skin

—*No, don't you tap my hand,*
     *no, go away—talk to yourself. . . .*


after Sonnets XXI, XLII & LXXVIII

## MISTRESS UMLAUT

dances on the slightest blemish,
the one
  freckling your nose, actually,

her stiletto heel rooting
the cartilage while
  you proffer her your *Je m'excuse*. . . .

Demure, she peels the body's home
and slips fat
  from the kidneys—sweet butter

to grease Fate's wheel. Long ago
it was,
  when sly Sisyphus loved her:

he handcuffed Hell to the Tartar throne,
cheating death
  so he could smother Madame

with kisses, and muck up her play
of Solitaire.
  —But if Hell couldn't do his work,

no one would die: the chopped-up soldier
strolled home
    for lunch, head splashing the table;

even the Gods, ever-bickering,
were struck dumb.
    So Mistress showers Sisyphus

with the marriage suit, dropping clubs
and diamonds
    on his head—how giddy he becomes!

until she takes out her tiny spoon
and flips
    a hearts-pebble he chases

downhill. Gathering like a snowball,
it rolls
    for years, down-a-down.

*If I can get blood from a stone,*
says
    Mistress Umlaut, her coal eyes flashing,

*then stone is my fruit.*

# MÖBIUS

for R. G.

As if sliding down the green, scuffed face
    of the wave, a seaplane falls
and turns together, keeping the waters of

the ear flat: a dead calm. But when the window's
    frowning strip of shoreline,
the battalions of tropical-drinks umbrellas

guarding the sandcastles and saltboxes
    of the rich,
when these flip upside down, and the pale

clouded sky floats below the ocean,
    then we jolt awake—
But this is not her dream, not water or land.

    *Tell me again, what illness do I think I have?*

The ropes of blood coil through her neck,
    they twist as it twists,
as the head looks for parents and young men,

for nurses, strangers, year upon year attending
    until the pulpy blood
knots up at last, and the warrens of

the brain dry and crackle, a town of names
    she saunters one long night:
streets without signs lead to a girlhood park,

to songs under stars, and lipstick,
    old houses forever
unbuilding themselves—but within the blue

jungle scaffolding, a gallery of faces
    stares back at her,
portraits she can't place . . . and then the town

flattens and crumbles behind her, it grows
    to dry scrabbled pasture
under a dishplate moon, hanging there

in the tints of the sky, yet like a stopped
    clock, right twice a day:

    *Now ma'am, can you remember the name of*
    *the President who was shot in the '60s?*

    *—Lincoln?*

And if the names had sunk beneath the sea,
    rolling hump and hollow,
leopard spotted foam—surgeons would haul up

the big sharks and club them silly, knife off a fin,
    then drop them
bleeding onto the docks of Alcatraz,

warning the inmates: "See that?
    No inside fin,
they'll swim round this Rock forever. . . ."

The convicts build the prison, then move inside,
    their block minds
ignite a thousand homes by dawn,

then melt in the butter sun of
    breakfast porridge. . . .
But this is not the Philosopher's circle prison,

no lidless Eye radiates from the center,
    beneficent
and watchful: the neutered grounds

here at the *Residence for Life*
    are groomed
like the campus of Depression State U:

past the dwarfish berms and drumlins
    a mazy cobalt
walkway slithers to the storage lake,

with its hooded fount of *aqua vitae* sudsing
    the green larvae,
its dry Gazebo Isle no one shuffles to . . .

One night, the distraught *Residence* cook
    shoots himself dead:
everyone mourns, but only the young staff

seek counseling, their threshold of death
    not yet raised
to that of teetering Mr. On-His-Toes,

of Ms. Wheelchair-With-Political-Bumper-Stickers,
    or elegant
Mrs. Whisper, polite confused survivors of

wiped-out families, trolley cars, jobs learned
    and lost, a cosmos
squeezed beneath the blood boulder—

*Why can't I remember my problem?*

They do not scream. They who once
    made things happen
now watch things happen to them:

they hand their middle chapters to
    their children,
and quietly appraise the spindle of

a leafless sapling outside, staked
    to three larger
poles of wood: all of them under arrest.

And you must calm yourself. In the acrid hold
    of their boat,
whose strangely knotted sail whips the wind

round on each side, anchorless boat
     that hugs the dock,
and keeps the dock from drifting to sea,

you can hear the first, reeling chapters,
     of pierside painters
crowding a rustic barrel-and-shanty scene

so clichéd the locals called it "Port Motif
     Number One"—:
the washy dab and smear of the medical test,

     *Can you tell me what day this is?*

     *—You mean now?*

The brush like an oar rinses off its paints;
     a filmy rainbow
upon the waters, coils and ribbons

you trace in your own sweet time.

## SURREY: WALLED GARDEN

The mower churns up crickets, they spray through
swordfern and hot poker; finches shepherd
the clicking troops to the brick loaf wall.
    July's cyclonic engine—

Onions bake in the soil, photos in the soft
glue albums curl. The garden lives only
for this year, its ranks of little poetries
    flower, gypsy pepper,

turk's turban gourd, espaliers of sweet pea,
and then, the tepid critic: *dwarf cosmos*.
The German gardener, pretty, jackbooted,
    bends to fill a bag

with swedes, as old Archie talks to her shoulder
about WW II rations and rainwater baths.
Victory garden, cold war garden, terror garden.
    It pays out—

Sixty years, a willow's age, since Archie found
the note a seamstress tucked inside his new overalls,
the quick Yorkshire girl who wrote on a dare,
    *I'd fancy a lad your size.*

They met, and married, here, standing on the lawn
three centuries old. She has set Archie's supper,
the morning's redbeet and cabbage, a slice
    of blue-veined cheese.

Tables of chance and paradise: gamblers
throw down spades and bones, gardeners cast down seeds—
they come a cropper, they come up deuces
    or daisies,

small grace at the bidding,
*Where art thou?*
&
    *Baby needs new shoes.*

## AGAINST THE GRAIN

for Joy Young


"My love is a read rose," you once told me.
Is love a tractor beam, a furrowed brow,
or simple as your name.
                                    Our little engine

is lugging words one stop past their station,
warm couplings stretch the sense. Can we talk straight?
An airplane's black box is orange;
                                    the orange

is green and unripe; the unready reader
thinks "naked to the waist" means *no pants*; she reads
"The sailors, stripped to the waist,
                                    swab the poopdeck"

and throws her book down. Hardy's drunken Mayor
of Casterbridge plays cards, bets his own wife
and loses her—
                    he's no Groucho, he repents,

spends his day selling *corn*, which in England
meant any grain, just as *deor* meant any beast
preying upon the heathlands,
                                    like the Latin

I prayed to, *trahit quemque sua voluptas,*
Virgil fingering the heart. I thought it meant
"whatever it is you love

                drags you onward."


A doom-magnet. Then you found the *Eclogues*
translation: wolf hunts goat, goat hunts clover;
*each was led by his liking—*

                not lovesick Dido


staggering through black woods, a wounded stag,
but slow bullocks hauling yoke and plow homeward. . . .
Our evenings, spent at puzzles

                and cross words;


even the house is semi-detached—let some
crackpot dictionary root us out. May I
call you, lying upon

                a German couch,


*Freud Jung*? (may I suggest *no pants*)—
Virgil stares at his pages, tears them up.
*Quis enim modus. . . .*


                What bound is set for love?

# COOK AT MAUI

Horseshoe beach and finger palm,
mist, small clouds, same rainbow, no albatross—
lovers oil their breasts, lazy from coconut
    milk, rum and sex,

the sun's narcosis—they hold murder in
their laps, books of broken empire, potboilers. . . .

Teens dive the waves' closing zero, old couples
    stagger from the foam,

as if the sea had taken our midlife,
the uncreative, absorptive waters
renewing their first world, which even now
    never looks to heaven—:

Noah sailed over drowned beasts and men; but
the Flood didn't drown the sea. Hog- and Unicorn-fish
still peck, from the cemeteries of brain-coral,
    the fruit of Genesis;

the century turtle seen by Captain Cook
still coasts the neap tide: centuries of foreplay,
rutting, abandonment, and no remorse—
    The breaching humpbacks,

the "Great Wings of New England," look east;
the novels, the *Decline of the West*, look east;
beach people, west of Eden, south of reason . . .

    Zero sea level

is never at zero's calm, but pitched, grabbing,
draining us—we're thrown off our rockers, lose
bearings like Captain Cook, who went loopy
    in the Bering Strait

and forced his crew to chew on walrus-fat—:
Tipping through the bathwaters of Hawaii,
the Captain ignored the local *politesse*;
    rather than take some islanders

hostage, and ask their cousins to return
his dinghy, Cook stormed the beach, a first world
Gen. MacArthur demanding hides. . . .
    The Elders brained him

and then, with cheery literalism,
the village gathered and cooked him up.

Green waterplates wash out; ribbons of white crepe
    pop in air; curving shore

and palm, sex curve of hip—the palm's gothic sway
that boys look for in cathedral statues, boys
who forgive the sinner and forget the sin.
    They tilt like York's

medieval spire . . .
                          Yorkshire: Cook's spawning grounds,
and Philip Larkin's home: the old man of Hull,
tipsy bookman with clicking teeth, athwart in
    a bedsit dreaming

the sex paradise he missed in '64—
his Girl on the Pill is gone now; our pills
thin the blood and sluice the kidney, or pickle
    the Mai Tai sugars.

So press a lemon-slice to your smile,
and watch the kayaks belly up. One ship still
waits in the shallows, like a hopeful dog.
    It is not Cook's boat,

not Bligh's, but Larkin's black sailed *Familiar*,
sloughing, mute. It is rigged for us:
No birds or Larkins in its wake. No waters
    that breed or break.

*Three*                              War Bird

# WAR BIRD: A JOURNAL
Poets' Anti-War Rally, February 12, 2003


The massed and pillared wings of
the White House never fly—
    whitewashed yearly, they stand
impervious

    to metaphor,

to hawk and dove, and red armies
of ants. Only the halting squirrels
    investigate, creeping past the arrowhead
gates to scratch

    the Midas lawns

for treasure— On the street, commentators
wander like boys in a story too simple
    to explain. The political message,
a hat

    punched inside out:

once, the Nazis got word that Churchill
would visit Roosevelt "in Casa Blanca":
    U-Boats bobbed near the Potomac,
waiting for him . . .

but Churchill,

as he said, was sailing to Morocco.
Reagan protesters splashed the Pentagon
    walls daily with cow blood—
soldiers waxed

    the plaster, and triremes

of rats licked the bloody grass;
the EPA sent health goons to stomp
    them, and the pacifists, away—
Then rats stormed

    the National Zoo:

urbane, patient inheritors of the earth,
they snapped prairie dogs like wishbones;
    vigilante zookeepers laced the ground
with poison,

    *Carthage delenda est,*

and killed the hippo. (Here, in the
New World Order, penguin and polar bear
    soak up ozone, and Nation shall
beat them both

    into plowshares. . . .)

Hawks and fat cats disdained
the White House squirrels, their proconsul
    Chevy Suburban nosed us aside:
we spoke

    against the war,

and for the cameras, spelled our names
on Chinese Radio—Elder poets shrewdly
    loitered at the lobbyist bar,
read first,

    then left us

to the falange of Secret Service men,
chatting like critics into their black
    lapels at every bungled line:
this was no

    singing school,

no falcon heard our crows and warbles . . .
Emily, our modest leader, rapped the gate:
    "Mrs. Bush wanted American poems—
I brought

    3,000,

all against the war. Can you take them?"
Gulping, the pimply guard asked his shirt
    for help; older hands hustled up,
"*The Great Oz*

    *cannot see you . . .*" etc.

Will four and twenty blackbirds fill
a cowboy hat? Bunkered belowdecks,
    the President goes for the burn,
racing the

    cut tongue

of his treadmill to a dead heat.
Even Nixon met the enemy once,
    strode with his staff into a red sea
of hippies—

    they didn't part,

and he burbled about baseball . . .
from his desk, he liked to watch
    the sightseers through a gap
in the hedges;

    peaceniks

learned this and blocked his view,
stood there day and night for years:
    Nixon, nightmare reality shanking
through his eyes,

    knelt with Kissinger:

*Henry*, he moaned, *what do they want?* . . .
Days from now, how many days,
    the Valentine "Woo at the Zoo" begins.
A hand-raised

    falcon bows,

and shares meat with its master. . . .
He bows in turn, and eats;
    both softly whisper *ee-chu*,
*ee-chu*,

    a duet

heard only on abstract and crumbling
cliffs—if a man were to stand or
    sing there, he'd fall. The master
straps on a

    a falcon feathered

courtesan's hat and turns away—
Flapping wildly, the falcon claws
    the head-shape, squawking,
gyrating to

    hold on,

imperial lunge and lunge,
biting at the skull it fed, as
    semen slowly drips into a
rubber dam.

# NOTES

"Jacopone *Pietà*: Justice": Jacopo dei Benedetti was a thirteenth-century Tuscan lawyer turned priest and poet. Known as Jacopone, he wrote more than ninety Lauds.

"American Incognito": Material on the war-wounded at Walter Reed Hospital, in Washington, D.C., is taken from *Washington Post* articles by Dana Priest and Anne Hull, published in February 2007. Material on mud storms in Iraq is taken from the *New York Times* article by Jim Dwyer published March 25, 2003. Mammoth information is taken from the Discovery Channel Web site (www.discovery.com). See also Zbigniew Herbert's essay "Securitas."

"War Bird": Falcon breeding information is taken from the National Zoo's magazine, *Zoogoer*.